CANONIC STUDIES

Bernhard Ziehn
(b. 20 Jan. 1845, Erfurt – d. 8 Sept. 1912, Chicago)

DEDICATED TO

Dr. and Mrs. Otto L. Schmidt

CHICAGO

CANONICAL STUDIES

A NEW TECHNIC IN COMPOSITION

CANONISCHE STUDIEN

EINE NEUE COMPOSITIONS-TECHNIK

VON

BERNHARD ZIEHN

Wm A. KAUN MUSIC CO., MILWAUKEE, WIS.

RICHARD KAUN MUSIK VERLAG, BERLIN, GER.

Title page of original 1912 edition

CANONIC STUDIES

Bernhard Ziehn

Edited and introduced
by Ronald Stevenson

CRESCENDO PUBLISHING, NEW YORK, N.Y.

This edition first published in the United States in 1977 by
Crescendo Publishing, New York.

Canonic Studies, under the title Canonical Studies, was first published in 1912 by Wm. A. Kaun Music Co., Milwaukee, Wis., USA and Richard Kaun Music Verlag, Berlin.

ISBN 0-87597-106-7

Printed in England

CONTENTS

INTRODUCTORY ESSAY

Bernhard Ziehn's contribution to the development of canon

by Ronald Stevenson

Apart from scant entries in standard reference books, there is little written on Bernhard Ziehn, either in German (his native language) or English (his adopted language). In English there is one article: Winthrop Sargeant's *Bernhard Ziehn, Precursor* (Musical Quarterly, April 1933). In German there are two sources of information: Busoni's essay *Die "Gotiker" von Chicago*, written in January 1910 for the German magazine *Signale* and reprinted in Busoni's selected essays, *Von der Einheit der Musik* (Max Hesses Verlag, Berlin, 1922)* – the "Gothics of Chicago" being Ziehn and his pupil Wilhelm Middelschulte. And the other German source is Hans Joachim Moser's monograph *Bernhard Ziehn/der deutsch-amerikanische Musiktheoretiker* (Verlag Julius Steeger, Bayreuth, 1950).

Bernhard Ziehn was born on 20th January 1845, a shoemaker's son. It is fitting that his birthplace was in Erfurt, Thuringia (Eastern Germany, formerly upper Saxony) because Erfurt was one of the headquarters of the Bach family and a Mecca for contrapuntists between 1650 and 1750. Johann Pachelbel worked there during Bach's childhood and taught, among many other pupils, Bach's eldest brother and first teacher. One of Bach's last pupils, Johann Christian Kittel, was also an Erfurter and this Bachian pedagogical lineage was continued, through Michael Gotthard Fischer and his pupil A.G. Ritter, down to the Erfurt boyhood of Bernhard Ziehn. Fétis relates how Kittel, as a mark of approval of his pupils' work, would draw aside a curtain and allow them a view of the life-size portrait of Bach which was his prized possession. Ziehn, too, in his work as teacher of counterpoint, metaphorically drew aside a curtain from a portrait of Bach – but a Bach with finger indicating the future.

Ziehn began, as Bach had finished, by being a school teacher. After studying at the teachers' seminary in Erfurt, Ziehn taught

* New, enlarged edition: *Wesen und Einheit der Musik*, revised by Joachim Herrmann (Max Hesses Verlag, Berlin-Halensee, 1956).

for three years in Mühlhausen, another Thuringian town of Bachian associations. Then in 1868 he emigrated to the United States where he taught music theory, mathematics and German at the German Lutheran School in Chicago (1868-71). During the 1870's he was synagogue organist in Chicago. Later he pursued private teaching and gradually established himself as a theorist. His pupils included some outstanding American composers, notably John Alden Carpenter.

Though living the rest of his life in America, he kept contact with Germany by contributing many articles for German music journals; articles characterised by a flair for polemic in which his chief adversary was Hugo Riemann. In addition to these articles, he published five books: *System der Übungen fur Clavierspieler* (1881); *Ein Lehrgang fur den ersten Clavierunterricht* (1881); *Harmonie – und – Modulationslehre* (1887; 2nd edition 1909); *Five and Six-Part Harmonies* (1911; containing 800 music examples); and the present volume, which appeared originally under the title *Canonical Studies/A New Technic in Composition* (1912). In the present reprint the title has been slightly changed to *Canonic Studies*. This final volume was published posthumously and was proof-read and seen through the Press by Ziehn's pupil Julius Gold. Ziehn died in Chicago on 8 September 1912.

In a letter to Julius Gold, written on 10 January 1912, Ziehn opined: "Not the laws of physics but the masterpieces of music are the standard of judgment for the science of music". This view demonstrates Ziehn's staunch opposition to that of nearly all theorists contemporaneous with him, who, supported by Helmholtz's researches, attempted to base harmonic theory on acoustic phenomena. Ziehn accepted a tempered chromatic-enharmonic basis for his system of harmony and developed Kirnberger's theory that all possible chords are reducible to the theory of adjacent thirds. In this way, Ziehn indicated connections between triadic and quartal harmony, whereas other theorists have regarded the two methods of chord construction as mutually exclusive. That is, harmony built on thirds has been regarded as traditional and harmony built on fourths as 'modern' (as exemplified in works by Scriabin and Schoenberg written about 1908). A quotation from a composition of my own, the opening Chorale-Prelude of my *20th Century Music Diary* for piano, demonstrates Ziehn's concept of the enharmonic unity of triadic and quartal harmony:

Ex.1 A 20th Century Music Diary (1959) Ronald Stevenson

The first and third chords here are identical but the first is notated as being built in 3rds and the third chord as being built in 4ths. The notation, with its enharmonic differences, indicates the resolution in each case. Dr. Nicolas Slonimsky has written that "Ziehn's 'enharmonic law', built on the principle of functional equality of chords, is an original contribution to the theory of harmony."

To return for a moment to Erfurt. Moser, in his monograph on Ziehn, describes Erfurt as the city of possibly the most beautiful cathedral steps in Germany and also refers to the noble architecture of the Luther University and the Augustinian cloisters; and Erfurt is also the city of flowers, the German Haarlem. It was perhaps no accident, as Moser again points out (*op.cit.*), that, after music, Ziehn's passion was botany. A Linné-like ability for classification was applied by Ziehn, not only to his botanical studies but to his music analysis. He codified a new classification of chromatic harmony.

In the *Allgemeine Musik-Zeitung* for 10-17 July 1903, he published an analysis of the first chord of Bruckner's 9th Symphony, described by German critics as *Unikum*, and showed that this chord had been used 400 years earlier by Henry VI in his *Et in Terra*; by Pergolesi; by Wilhelm Friedemann Bach and by Beethoven. Ziehn was Bruckner's first apostle in America, years before the present *Brucknerindustrie*.

Ziehn found the whole-tone scale, not only in the French Impressionists and in Liszt, but in the finale of Schubert's Octet op. 166 (*vide* Schubert's Collected Works II, p.57, 6 bars before letter G). And Ziehn's resolution of the whole-tone chord in his *Harmonie – und – Modulationslehre* of 1887 is identical with that in Schoenberg's *Harmonielehre* of 1911 – almost a quarter of a century later!

But Ziehn's *opus ultimum, Canonic Studies,* is the chief reason for his continued significance. This work postulates that canonic writing need not be limited to simple diatonic harmony, but may, and – for its complete development – indeed *must*, entail a chromatic-enharmonic system of harmonisation transcending classical concepts of tonality.

The subtitle to the first (American) edition – "A New Technic of Composition" – shows that Ziehn's intention was to address himself not only to students writing academic exercises, but to composers writing music. The etymology of the verb "to compose" (from the French *com* –, with, and *poser*, from late Latin *pausare*, to place) indicates that composition is the art and craft of putting musical ideas together. Canon (from the Greek, *kanon*, rule, that is, composition according to rule) is the most essential form of contrapuntal composition, because it is concerned with putting a melody together with (or against) itself. Canonic imitation is the common factor in counterpoint of different periods and styles, from the canons of the Netherlands School, to the Palestrinian motet, the Purcellian fantasy, the Bachian or Handelian Invention and Fugue, or the Fugues of Haydn, Mozart, Beethoven, Reicha, Mendelssohn, Schumann, Brahms, Reger, Busoni, Hindemith, Shostakovich or Britten.

In my book *Western Music/an Introduction* (Kahn & Averill, London, 1971) I draw an analogy between canon and a person walking with his shadow: the person representing the musical subject; the shadow representing the canonic imitation. Extending the metaphor, we might say canon by augmentation (a subject answered by itself in longer notes) is like a person walking with his lengthened shadow. And canon by diminution (a subject answered by itself in shorter notes) is like a person walking with his foreshortened shadow.

Canon *in moto perpetuo* avoids a final cadence but repeats *ad infinitum* (or *ad nauseam*).

The answering voice or voices of a canon may be at any interval from the original pitch of the subject. Every third variation in Bach's "Goldberg" Variations for keyboard is a canon; each successive one at the interval of one degree wider than the previous one, beginning with canon at the unison (an exact replica-answer) and ending with canon at the 9th. The "Goldberg" Variations are the keystone of canonic writing. They should be studied by practising them slowly (so that their counterpoint may be heard more clearly), preferably in a comparative study of the editions of Busoni (Breitkopf, Leipzig/Wiesbaden) and of Ralph Kirkpatrick (Schirmer, N.Y.). I suggest than an instructive exercise would be for the student to make symmetrical inversions of Bach's Variations 3, 6, 9, 12, 15, 18, 21, 24 and 27, after having read the basic principles of symmetrical inversion elucidated on Ziehn's opening pages. In that way he would creep inside the cavernous creative process of Bach's mind and would prepare himself also for what Ziehn has to impart later in this book. Here is the opening of Bach's first canonic variation, with its symmetrical inversion (not to be played simultaneously!):

Canon should not be thought of as artifice. Who made the first canon? Was it not the primitive who heard the echo of his rudimentary song? For canonic music is echo-music. And in the hands of the master – as in Bach's "Goldberg" Variations – canon is as natural in music as echo is in nature.

Of course, canon, like the antique personification of Echo, has been wrapped up in myth and mystery. The 15th century masters of the second Netherlands School, Okeghem and Obrecht, and Okeghem's pupil Josquin des Prez, loved to set puzzles in the form of enigmatic canons. These would consist of the musical subject adorned by some cryptogram – maybe a cross or a hand or a Latin tag – which had to be solved before the canon could be worked out. These conundrums persisted into the 16th century: there is an example in Thomas Morley's *A Plaine and Easie Introduction to Practicall Musicke* (1597). As a canon, it is neither "plain" nor "easy" (see examples 7 and 7a at the end of this essay).

But more often canon has been written more rapidly and playfully as a souvenir of some convivial occasion, as when Kuhlau visited Beethoven in Baden in September 1825, as Thayer recounts in his Beethoven biography: "Beethoven seems to have held his own in the van of the revel. He wrote a canon in the conversation book with B–A–C–H (B flat - A - C - B natural) as an opening motive and the words 'Kuhl, nicht lau' (Cool, not lukewarm) – a feeble play on the Danish musician's name, but one which served to carry the music." This kind of sportive canon is like a musical pun.

Even Bach mixes together two German folk tunes in the Quodlibet near the end of his sublime "Goldberg" Variations, as though for all the world he were mixing punch!

I very much like some words Ezra Pound writes in his book *ABC of Reading*: "Gloom and solemnity are entirely out of place in even the most rigorous study of an art originally intended to make glad the heart of man." Many books on counterpoint groan under their bulk of verbiage. And the student groans even more. Not so with Ziehn's book.

There is a fundamental difference between Ziehn's methodology as theorist and that of all the other major theorists of counterpoint from the 16th to the 20th century, from Zarlino and Zacconi to Morley, Fux, Marpurg, Albrechtsberger, Sechter, Cherubini, Fétis, Taneiev, and Jeppesen. They all present more pages of text than of musical examples, whereas Ziehn's work consists mainly of music, with a minimum of verbal explanation. Some of the earlier theorists, including Morley and Fux, interlard their texts with supplications and "prayers before labour", calculated to equate counterpoint with the fear of God! And Taneiev's *Convertible Counterpoint in the Strict Style* (1906) presents his thesis algebraically, with pages of equations. All these works are of much historical importance and certainly of practical use, even though some of them (particularly Fux and Albrechtsberger) are riddled with misconceptions as to what constituted Palestrinian practice. Even so, Fux's *Gradus ad*

Parnassum was the *vade mecum* for Haydn, Mozart and Beethoven.

Another difference between Ziehn and all other theorists is that, whereas their intention (not always achieved) was to codify past practice, Ziehn was exploring new paths. The principle innovation of *Canonic Studies* is the theory and practice of symmetrical inversion. This concept, first formulated by Ziehn in 1876, postulates a chromatic application of the old *contrarium reversum.*

In the annotations appended to Fugue VIII (32) in Part II, Book 2 of his edition of the *Wohltemperiertes Klavier*, Busoni traces the technique of symmetrical inversion from Bach to Ziehn. As the simplest example of the principle, he gives a two-part canon over a free bass from Bach's Canonic Variations on "Von Himmel hoch da komm' ich her":

Ex.3 Canonic Variations: "Von Himmel hoch" Bach

This is, of course, the "mirror" canon which Busoni describes as like a reflection in water (*Wasserspiegelung*): a vertical turning upside-down; inversion in space. He goes on to explain the *cancrizans* or "crab" canon as horizontal inversion in time. And he points out the essential unmusicality of the "crab" canon: "for the ear, and equally for the eye, it is incomprehensible, as if one were to read the word Organismus as 'Sumsinagro'." If a "crab" canon makes music, it does so despite its carapaceous form.

As an example of how music by Bach may yield developments which Bach himself did not explore, Busoni quotes (*op.cit.*) from his own *Fantasia Contrappuntistica*, which embodies a completion of Bach's incomplete triple fugue from *Die Kunst der Fuge;* and this quotation is given as an example of symmetrical inversion of a canon harmonised in 3rds and 6ths:

Ex.4 Fantasia Contrappuntistica **Busoni**

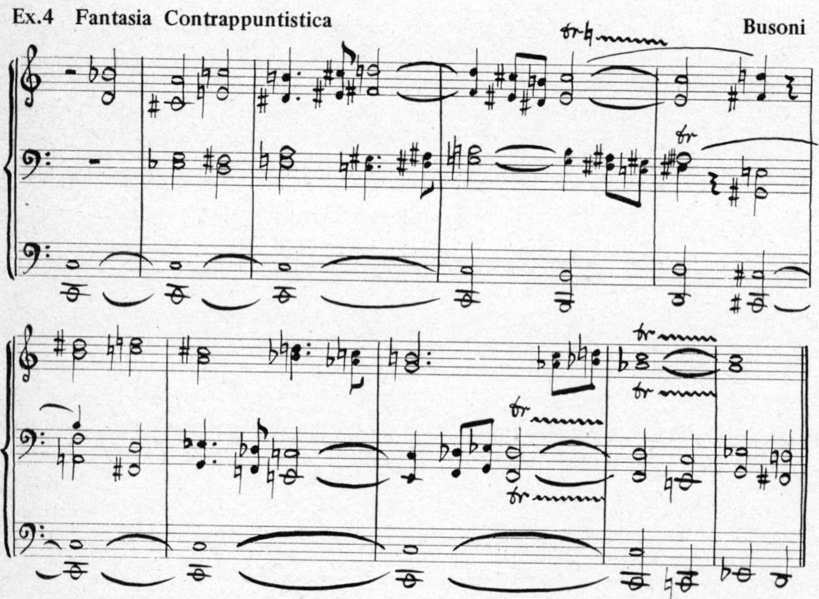

In a footnote to the *Kleine Ausgabe* (1912) of the *Fantasia Contrappuntistica,* Busoni acknowledges his indebtedness to Bernhard Ziehn for suggesting the combination of the first subject of the *Kunst der Fuge* with the three subjects of the triple fugue as being the "missing link" in Bach's incomplete final work; and the *edizione definitiva* of the Busoni work (1910)

is dedicated "*An Wilhelm Middelschulte, Meister des Kontrapunktes*" (Middelschulte was Ziehn's favourite pupil).

Example 4 may be compared with other examples of canon harmonised in 3rds or 6ths given in the section towards the end of this volume, *Canonic elaboration of a short motive.* And a side-study to this material might be the Fugue in Paderewski's Piano Sonata in E flat minor, op.21 (Bote-Bock, Berlin, 1903), a two-part fugue with each part harmonised in double 3rds or 6ths, fusing two-part counterpoint with four-part harmony.

There are many connections between ideas in Ziehn's *Canonic Studies* and 20th century music. His tables of modes given on the early pages invite comparison with the unusual modes suggested by Busoni in his *New Aesthetic* (1906)* and incorporated in his *Elegy no. 6* for piano (Breitkopf, Leipzig, 1908); and also with John Foulds' *Essays in the Modes* for piano (Senart, Paris, 1928) and many works of Olivier Messiaen.

The principle of "progressive tonality" (the term coined by Robert Simpson to describe a composition which begins in one tonality, progresses through different keys or tonal centres and ends in a tonality different from the opening one), found in the Symphonies of Carl Nielsen and of Robert Simpson and others, is endorsed, as it were, by many of Ziehn's examples.

Bartók availed himself of Ziehn's symmetrical inversion, as may be seen in *Dragons' Dance* from Book 3 of *Mikrokosmos* for piano (Boosey & Hawkes, London 1940):

* Reprinted in *Three Classics in the Aesthetics of Music*: Debussy/Busoni/Ives (Dover paperback, N.Y. 1962).

Symmetrical inversion produces harmony through counterpoint. The principle can be applied even where the counterpoint is minimal, as in the following quotation from the Rumanian-Italian composer Roman Vlad (born 1919):

Ex.6 Cantata: Le Ciel est Vide (1953) Roman Vlad

Many more examples might be given of 20th century music which corroborates Ziehn's thesis; but they would only labour points already made.

My responsibilities as an editor have been to abridge the original book slightly by omitting additional music examples; at the same time exercising care to retain at least one example of each technique demonstrated. I have also anglicised some of Ziehn's teutonicisms and the German text which was originally printed alongside the English text, has been omitted.

In remembering Ziehn we should not forget his wife, Emma, whom he married in America and whose devotion to the man and his work motivated her activities until her death in Chicago in 1921.* It was she who deposited copies of the posthumously published *Canonic Studies* with Busoni and other musicians, ensuring that the seed would not fall on barren soil.

* The Ziehns had two children: a daughter who died young and a son who lived long and worked as a doctor of medicine in Chicago.

Ex.7 **Morley**

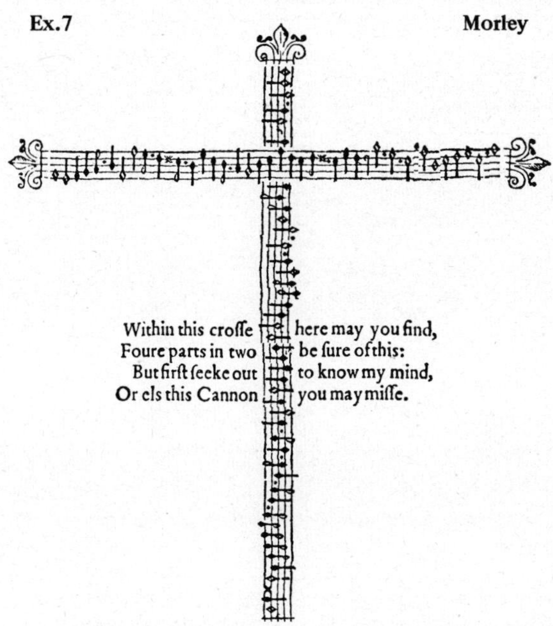

Ex.7a Enigmatic Canon (solution of ex.7) **Morley**

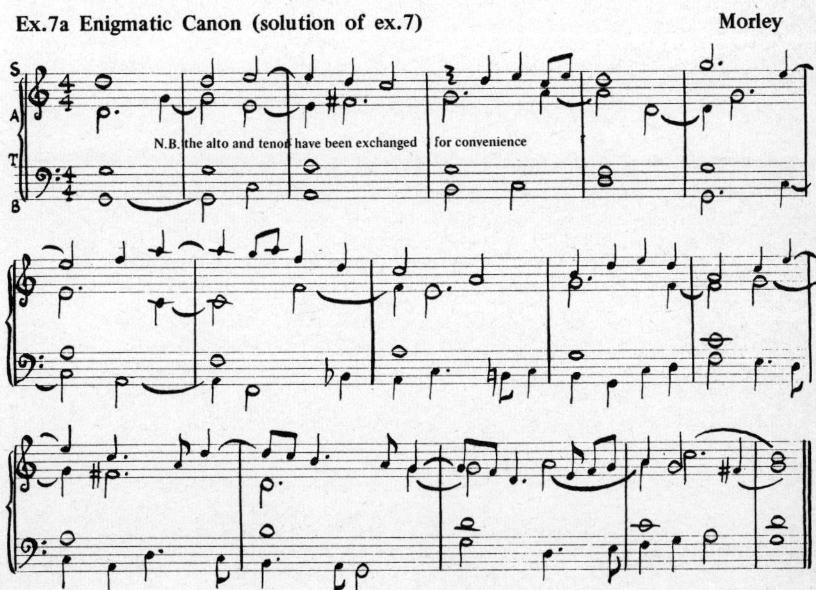

A SELECTED, CHRONOLOGICAL BIBLIOGRAPHY

For further study in performance

Compiled by the editor

1 Josquin des Prez (c. 1445-1521) : *A l'heure que je vous p.x.* canon for 4 instruments (1503, reprinted in *Geschichte der Musik in Beispielen,* ed. Schering, Breitkopf, Leipzig, 1962)

2 Thomas Tallis (c. 1515-85) : *Canon for 4 voices ("Tallis's Canon")* : 2-part canon with 2 free parts (Archbishop Parker's Psalter, London, 1567; reprinted in many hymnals)

3 Giovanni Pierluigi da Palestrina (1525-94) : *Missa ad Fugam* : double canon; *Sacerdotes Domini*; *Sine Nomine* : canons on all degrees of the mode and at various time-intervals (1601, Venice, reprinted in the Breitkopf collected edition)

4 William Byrd (1542-1623) : *Diliges Dominum* : canon for 8 voices (4 simultaneous canons, each pair of voices singing the retrograde of each other). (Ed. Fellowes, OUP, London, 1927)

5 Johann Sebastian Bach (1685-1750) : "*Goldberg*" *Variations* for keyboard (1742, Schmid, Nurenberg; ed. Busoni, for piano, Breitkopf, 1915; ed. Kirkpatrick, for harpsichord, Schirmer, NY, 1938)

: *Canonic Variations & Fugue from "The Musical Offering"* on a theme of Frederick the Great (1747; solution and piano version by Busoni, Breitkopf, 1916)

6 Wolfgang Amadeus Mozart (1756-91) : 29 Canons listed in the Köchel Catalogue, Section X of Index (Breitkopf)

7 Ludwig van Beethoven (1770-1827) : "*Mir ist so wunderbar*" : canon for 4 voices with orchestra, from the opera *Fidelio*, act 1, no 3 (1805; first ed. Cappi, Vienna, 1807; vocal score by Roth, Boosey & Hawkes, London, 1948)

8 Robert Schumann (1810-56) : *6 Studies in canon-form* for pedal piano (or piano duet or organ), op 56 (Breitkopf, 1845)

9 Cesar Franck (1822-90) : *Finale from Sonata for violin and piano* (Hamelle, Paris, 1886)

10 Max Reger (1873-1916) : *Duos, Canons & Fugues for violins,* op 131, set 2 (Breitkopf, 1914)

11 Gustav Holst (1874-1934) : *Terzetto for flute, oboe and viola* : polytonal (Chester, London, 1925)

: *6 Canons for equal voices,* unaccompanied: polytonal. Words translated from the Latin by Helen Waddell. (1932; Faber, London, 1967).

: *2 Canons for equal voices and piano.* (1932; Faber, London, 1967)

12 Paul Hindemith (1895-1963) : no 11 of *Ludus Tonalis for piano* : fugue in canon (Schott, London, 1943)

13 Luigi Dallapiccola (1904-74) : *Sonatina Canonica for piano* (Suvini Zerboni, Milan, first ed. 1946; 2nd ed. 1950; 3rd ed. 1953)

14 Fritz Joede (editor) : *Der Kanon* (anthology). (Moseler, Wolfenbuttel, 1948 : London agent, Novello)

Acknowledgements

The music examples quoted in the introductory essay are reproduced by courtesy of the following publishers:

Busoni's *Fantasia Contrappuntistica* : Breitkopf & Hartel, Leipzig/Wiesbaden

Bartok's *Dragons' Dance* : Boosey & Hawkes, London
Vlad's *Le Ciel est Vide* : Suvini Zerboni, Milan

Scales symmetrically inverted

D Dorian Hungarian D maj. D Aeolian D Mixolydian D Phrygian D Ionian

D Dorian Hungarian D maj. Mixolydian D Aeolian D Ionian D Phrygian

In the lower row of the following sets the scales are arranged in the manner of the ancient Greek modes, i.e. from fifth to fifth descending.

"Authentic" modes become "plagal."

Scales with chromatic by-tones.

Symmetrically correspond: minor sixth and major seventh, major sixth and minor seventh, minor second and augmented fourth.

In nos 3—8 the sixth in the major scale is minor, because the seventh in the minor scale is major.

1. D min. with 2 sevenths 2. D maj. with 2 sixths

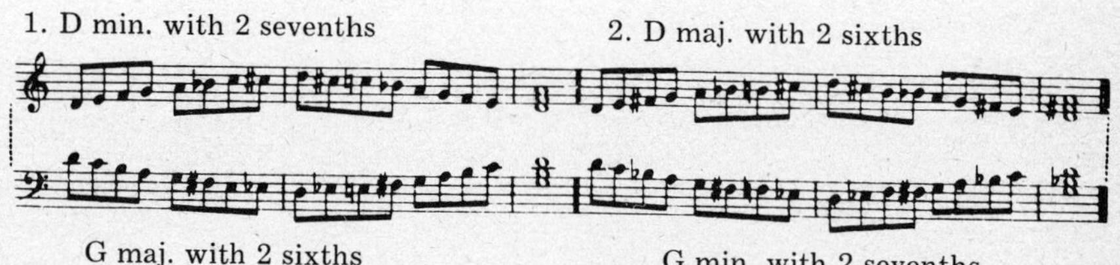

G maj. with 2 sixths G min. with 2 sevenths

3. D min. with 2 sixths

4. D maj. with 2 sevenths

G maj. with 2 sevenths

G min. with 2 sixths

5. D min with 2 fourths

6. D maj. with 2 seconds

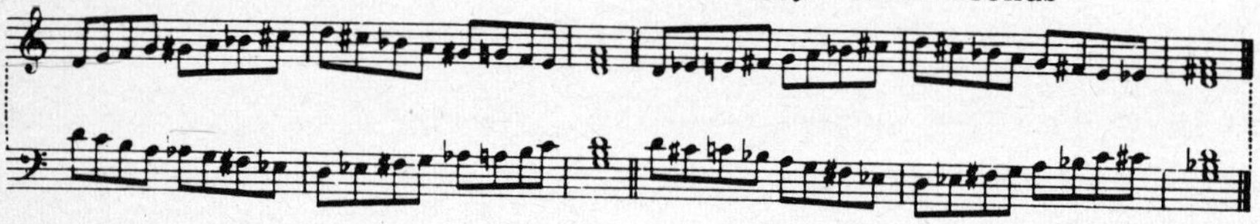

G maj. with 2 seconds

G min. with 2 fourths

7. D min with 2 seconds

8. D maj. with 2 fourths

G maj. with 2 fourths

G min. with 2 seconds

Repetition of nos 3—8, but in major with major sixth instead of minor sixth, and in minor with minor seventh instead of major seventh.

Two additional tones

1. D maj. with 2 sixths & 2 sevenths

2. D min. with 2 sixths & 2 sevenths

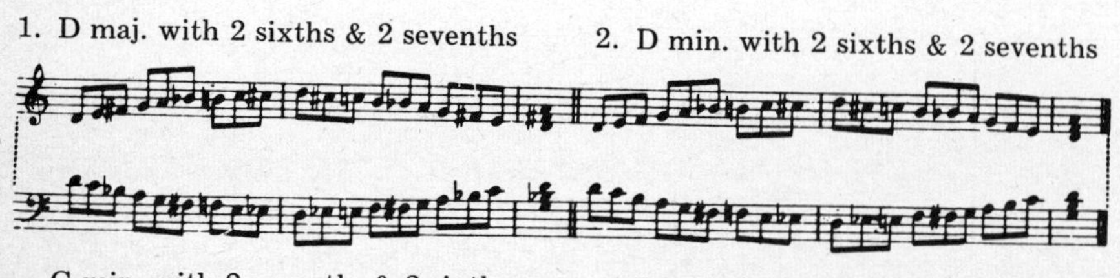

G min. with 2 sevenths & 2 sixths

G maj. with 2 sevenths & 2 sixths

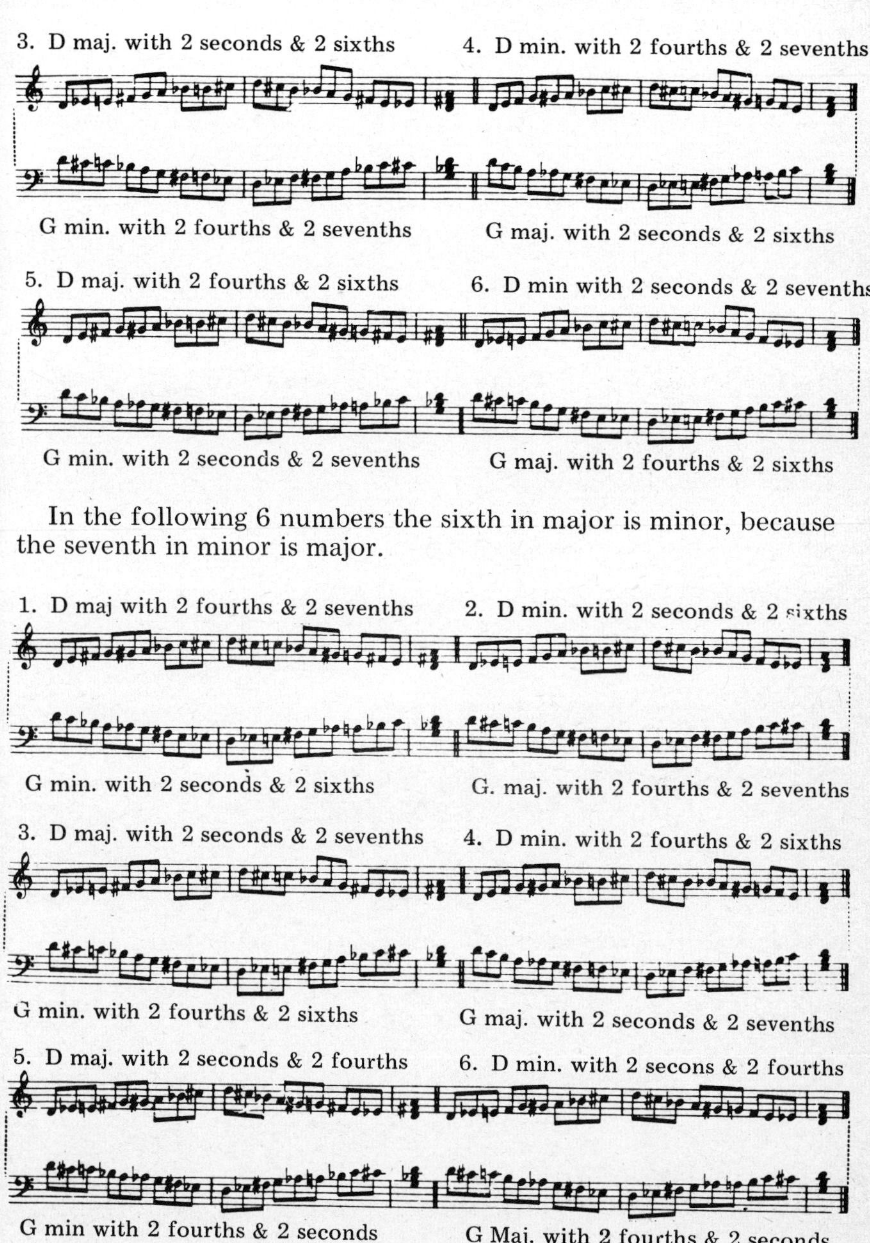

In the following 6 numbers the sixth in major is minor, because the seventh in minor is major.

Repetition of the last 6 examples, but in major, major sixth instead of minor sixth, and in minor, minor seventh instead of major seventh.

The whole-tone scale

Suspensions from above become suspension from below, and vice versa

A triad in octave-position becomes a triad in second inversion.

The doubling of the fundamental tone in seventh-chords becomes doubling of the seventh.

In the seventh-chord the leaping fundamental tone becomes leaping seventh.

A few short settings and their symmetrical inversion will illustrate the subject clearly.

Experience gained by careful practice is the only means of finding out whether or not a setting is suitable for symmetrical inversion. No rules can be given, but with certainty we can say: the more chromatic a setting is the more appropriate it becomes for symmetrical inversion, because chromatic progression is the smoothest. We must learn, that there are more both useful and well-sounding harmonies and chord progressions than are dreamt of in magisterial wisdom, whether old or new. We must learn as much as possible about accidental dissonances, and must try to think in the double counterpoint of the octave, that is to imagine a composition with interchangeable parts.

Most of the larger sized canons are meant in tempo tranquillo.

A fermata (hold) near the end of a canon designates an earlier close.

Ties occasionally given are not legato ties; they only show the compass of the themes.

A few model canons by John A. Carpenter and Otto Wolf, pupils of mine, are given in addition to my own work.

Canons in the octave and prime

The triad

In this section C major and A minor stand also for C minor and A major.

In two parts

Symmetrical inversion

Symmetrical inversion

Dominant and minor seventh-chords

In the 3rd and 5th examples the last chord is "free", that means, it is not thematic.

Symmetrical inversion

The major ninth-chord

in symmetrical inversion

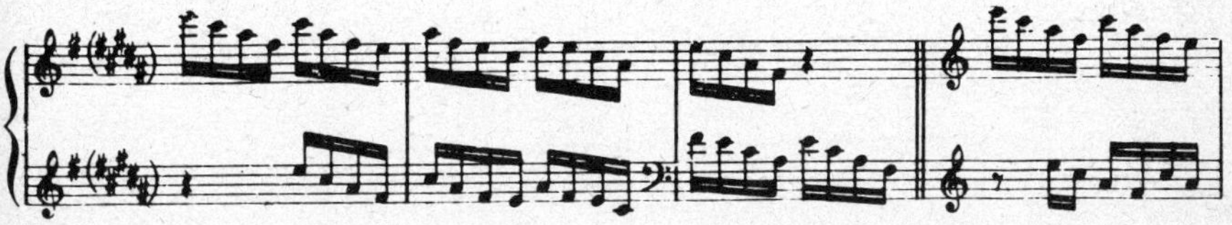

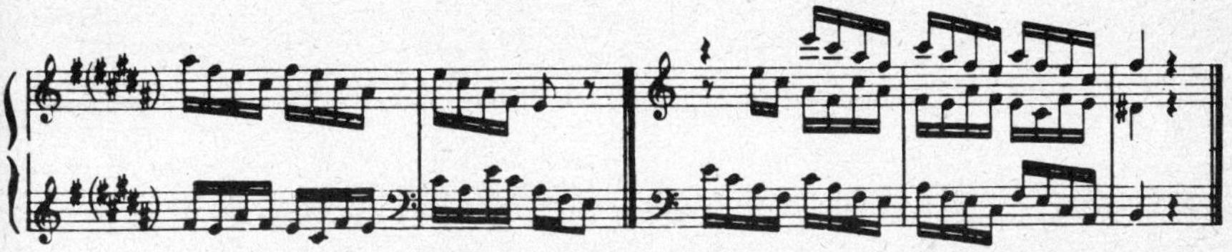

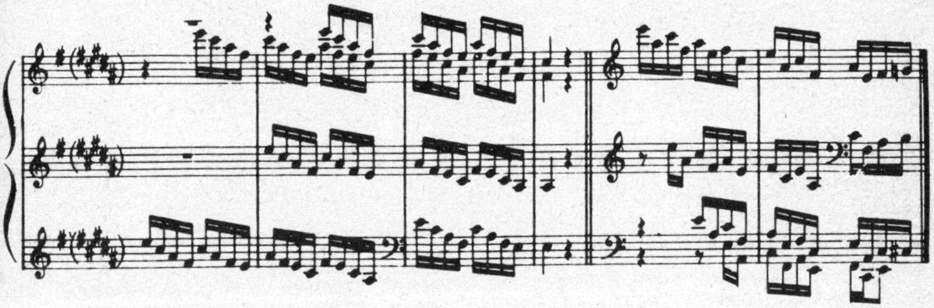

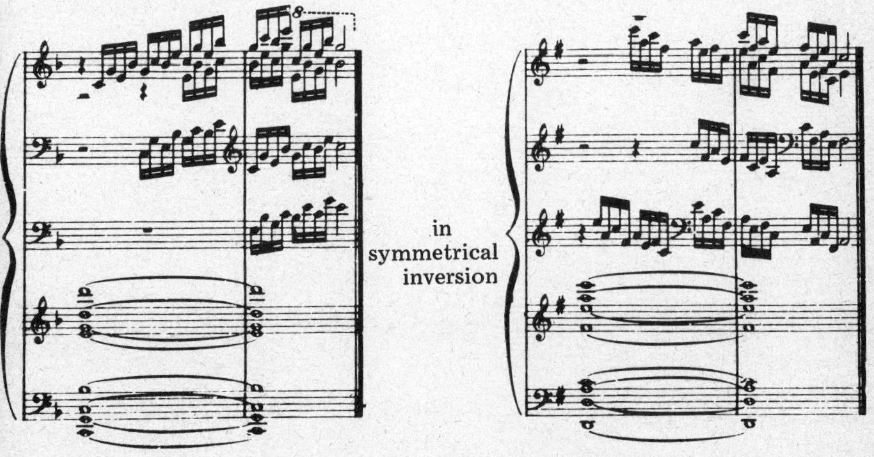

The triad with accidental dissonances

The sixth before the fifth.

The augmented fourth before the fifth

Symmetrically

The lower second before the prime.

The minor second before the prime.

The fourth before the third.

The augmented second
before the third
The Second between prime and third
also D major
also G minor
Also the D major, B♭ major, B minor
G major and G minor triads similar to
the last three examples

Symmetrical inversion of the preceding examples

The last two examples are the sym. inv. of the preceding two.

For the sake of brevitiy, from here on, the letters A and B designate the original form and its sym. inv.

More and extended examples

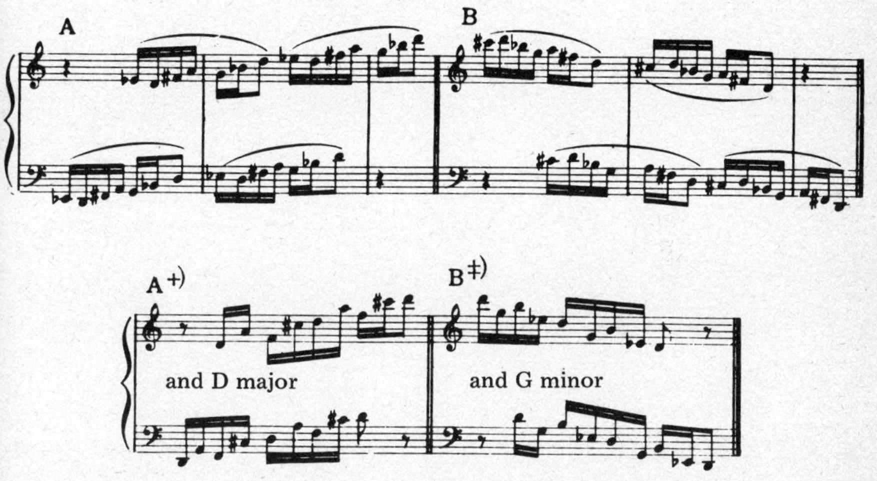

+) also without the ♯ before c, but with the signature of G major, A minor, or C minor.
†) also without the ♭ before e, but with the signature of D minor, C major, or A major.

A
B
A
B
A
B

In the first three of the following examples *f*# may take the place of *f*. But neither in major nor minor are they suitable for symmetrical inversion.

After sufficient study all examples in this chapter may be transposed.

A

and C minor

B

and A major

A

and A major

B

and C minor

A
and C min.
and F min.
B
and A maj.
and E maj.
A
Also with e♭ instead of e
B
also with c♯ instead of c
A
B

Seventh-chords with accidental dissonances

With suspensions

+) free cadence

With passing tones

A

B

A

B

supplementary part

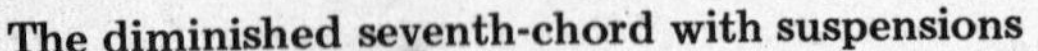

The diminished seventh-chord with suspensions

In two parts

In three parts

With a supplementary part and a free close

The following canon is in some respect a double canon, because the lower parts are not entirely equal to the upper parts: in the bass and tenor suspensions from below, and in the soprano and alto suspension from above. Free close.

In four parts

A

B

The four parts of a given setting melodically arranged in one part, thus becoming the theme of a *canon in the octave.*

2.

3.

4.

5.

Of the following canon in the prime and octave *the two closing bars* are considered *the given setting.*

Canon in the prime

Theme of 16 bars

B

Cannon in the prime and the octave

The 2nd half with symmetrically inverted theme. Section B is the symmetrical inversion of section A.

Canons in the fourth and the fifth

8 Canons developed from a short theme

b)
3.
a)

b)
4.
a)

b)

Six canons in the fourth

developed from a short theme

One and the same canon with different part-entries

1.

Two elaborations of the same theme

2.

3. (Variation of no. 2)

Three more elaborations

In the course of the canon the theme varies several times.

Ten Canons in the fifth and the fourth developed from a more extensive theme..

2

3

4

5. A.

5. B.

6. A.

6. B.

Variations of canons 6A and 6B
All parts begin at the same time.

Canons in the fifth
(lower fourth)
Theme of 8 bars

The first 4 bars of the theme are after the 3rd theme of the unfinished fugue in Bach's "Kunst der Fuge"

Both halves of the theme beginning simultaneiously

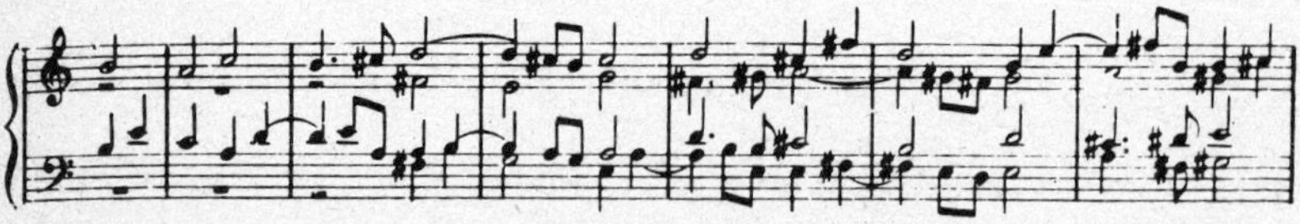

and so on as before

2.

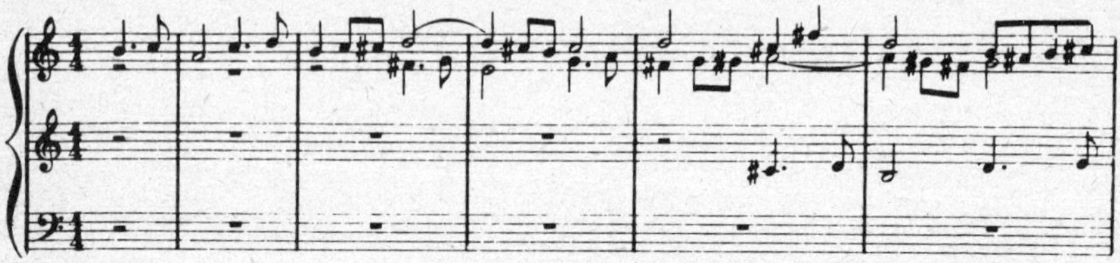

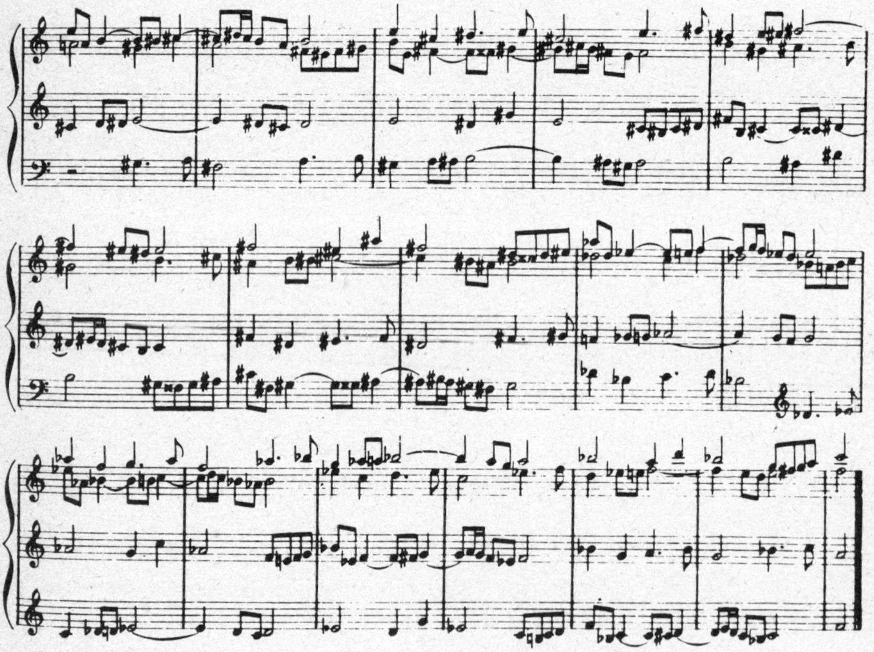

Here also both halves of the theme may begin simultaneously.

and so on see above

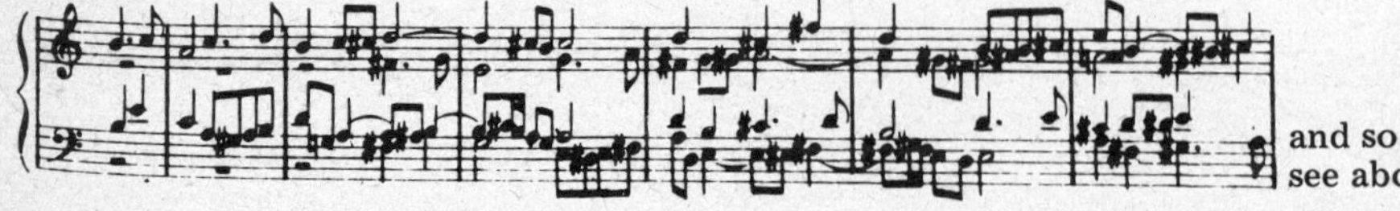

Two Canons in the fifth and their symmetrical inversion

(Canons in the lower fifth)

Theme of 12 bars

The first 3 bars of the theme are after the theme of the first C major fugue in Bach's Welltempered Clavier.

1. B.

2. A.

2. B.

Three canons in the fifth or fourth on other themes

1) Canon in the fifth
Theme of 4 bars.

3) Canon in the fifth
Theme of 4 bars

a)

b) The repetition of the theme in the same part occurs a minor sixth lower instead of a major third higher.

c) Different arrangement of parts

d) The minor scale with minor second instead of the major scale with minor second and minor sixth, in the beginning of the theme

Five-part *Canon in the Fifth*

Theme of 10 bars

Two Canons of which the 2nd half is the sym.inv. of the 1st half

1) Theme of 4 bars

2) Theme of 8 bars, of which the first two are the theme of a fugue by Otterstrom.

Free: in section A the last note in the bass, and in section B the last note in the soprano.

Five canons with continuous themes

1) Canon in the fifth

2) Canon in the fourth (lower fifth)

Free: the last note in the bass

3) Canon in the fifth

Free: the last note in the alto and tenor.

4) Canon in the fourth

5) Canon in the fifth
(Symmetrical inversion of No 4)

Diminished seventh-chords chromatically progressing carried out in double-canons in the fifth or fourth.

3. A
4. A
3. B
4. B
5. A
6. A

5. B

6. B

7. A

7. B

The following double-canons are also based on diminished seventh-chords in chromatic progression.

free

Chromatic double-canon in the major sixth and the minor seventh. The 2nd half is the sym. inv. of the 1st half. In the cadence a few free notes.

After such and similar experiments it should not be difficult to invent double-canons without previous arrangement of chords.

Examples

Variation of canon A

Variation of canon B

Eight-part double-canon in the fourth

Both of the themes contain eight bars, and consist of two unequal sections. In both canons two parts begin with the first, and the other two parts with the second section.

John A. Carpenter

rit.
rit.
rit.

Eight-part quadruple canon in the fourth

Each of the four themes is eight bars long.

John A. Carpenter

Canons in the octave and fifth

A Sketch
Theme of 4 bars

3.
4.

5.
3
3
6.

Two six-part double canons

The following four-part canon can be combined with the one or the other two-part canon.
Both of them are in the fifth, and their themes are of four bars.

Canons in the octave and fifth (A) resp. Octave and fourth (B)

A variation of the preceding canons

Both canons may be ended at the hold

A canon in the fifth and octave with a continuous theme. The sketch, unmusical indeed, shows the construction.

Canons in the major second and minor seventh

If the whole-tone scale in a four-part setting is harmonized by chords of the same kind, one chord on each degree, and if the part-progression of the first two chords is transferred to every following pair of chords, the result will be a two part canon in the major second or minor seventh.

The tones of the whole-tone scale considered as thirds of minor triads, or the tones of the chromatic scale, two instead of one, considered as thirds of homonymous major and minor triads.

Nos A, 6 and 9 also with the chromatic scale in the bass, and Nos. B, 6 and 9, with the chromatic scale in the soprano. See Nos 1 & 2

12.
A
B
13.
A
14.
B
A
15.
B

16.
17.
A
B
A
18.
B
19.
20.
A
B

21.
A
B
22. A
23.
B
24.
A
B

25.
A.
B.
26.
A.
B.
27.
28.
A.
B.

29.
A.
B.
30.
A.
B.
A.
B.

Three-part canons in the major second and minor seventh

A sketch: the whole-tone scale harmonized by major or minor triads, two chords on one degree, in the circle of fifths. Only a few suggestions are given here. Elaborations similar to those in the preceding section.

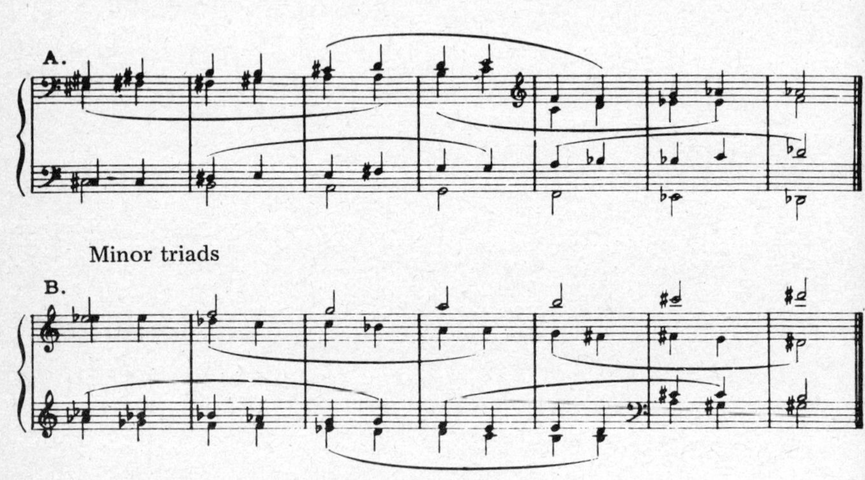

Homonymous minor and major alternating

Homonymous major and minor alternating

With accidental dissonances, e.g.

More florid by adding shorter notes, the scale with passing semitones.

Two four-part canons in the major second or minor seventh

Theme of 2 bars. Notes of equal value.

Two four-part canons in the minor seventh or major lower second (A), resp. minor lower seventh or major second (B).

The parts begin simultaneously. Theme of 32 bars.
Free: the 2nd crotchet of the closing chord.

B. Adagio

Three canons of which the second part is the symmetrical inversion of the first part.

OTTO WOLF

Variation of the preceding canon

B. Z.

Two six-part canons in the major second or minor seventh

Theme of 3 bars. Notes of equal value. (Free closing chord)

A.

B.
8

8

Six-part canon in the major second or minor lower seventh, with a continuous theme.

The first four bars are the theme of a fugue by Otterstrom.

1. Soprano
2. Soprano
Alto
Tenor
1. Bass

1. Soprano
2. Soprano
Alto
Tenor
1. Bass
2. Bass
free)

Two six-part double-canons in the minor seventh or major second.
The two four-part canons may also be taken separately as single canons.

Rudimentary sketch: every degree of the whole-tone scale harmonised with many chords repeated in the same order. The two two-part canons are additions formed by rhythmically and melodically different arrangement of chordic tones occurring on the corresponding beats.

The four-part canon has four bars; the two part canon two bars.

8
B.

Canons in the minor third and major sixth

If the chromatic scale in groups of three notes is uniformly harmonized, and if the part-progression in these groups is always the same, then, four-part setting presumed, three-part canons in the minor third or major sixth are the result.

The harmonies in the groups following each other are a minor third apart: a third lower, when the scale descends (as in nos. 1A, 2B, 3B and 4A); a third higher, when the scale ascends (as in nos. 1B, 2A, 3A and 4B).

[Minor third and major sixth occasionally appear in enharmonic change as augmented second and diminished seventh.]

The preceding four canons in retrograde inversion.

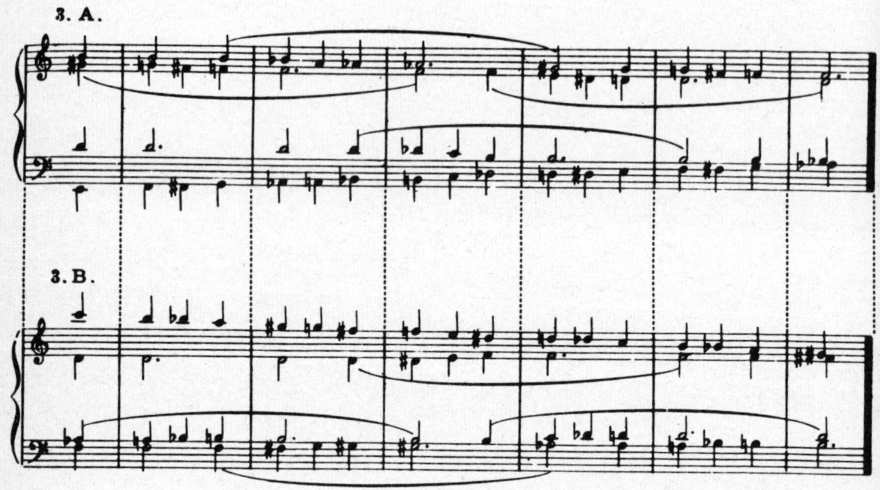

The four canons under A contain in every bar a dominant seventh-chord twice, and of its six enharmonic resolution chords the simplest one passing (that is the one with two tones common to both chords), resp. one of the enharmonic changes of a dominant seventh-chord and its simplest resoltuin. In the canons under B a minor seventh-chord takes the place of the dominant chord.

Certainly other chords may be chosen.

These short canons can be expanded by figuration. Rhythmical alterations of the scale may change the time. See the next two examples.

A few more canons founded upon the chromatic scale.

Parts enter after each other

The following 4 canons are entirely chromatic, and the scale is rhythmically altered.

B.

Parts enter after each other

Two three-part canons in the minor third.
A variation of the chromatic scale as supplementary part.

(free)
B. Adagio

As soon as one is capable of mastering this kind of canon, one should try to compose canons of more than three parts, and without the aid of the chromatic scale. The following collection of canons: two of four parts, three of five, and one of six parts, two six-part double-canons, two nine-part triple-canons, and one of seven parts, may serve as examples.

Two four-part canons in the minor third.

In canons of this kind the repetition of the theme occurs on the same degree in the same part.

Five-part canon in the minor third

The theme is 10 bars long

A variation of the same.

Five- or six-part canon in the major sixth (minor lower third).

The first two bars of the theme are the theme of a fugue by Otterstrom.

Or of 6 parts beginning at the last quaver of the 10th bar

Two nine-part triple-canons in the minor third

Each of the three-part canons has three bars and ascends. The lower canon is chromatic.

The lower and the inner canon together can be considered as an independent double- canon of six parts.

(free)
(free)

In the following symmetrical inversion the arrangement of the three canons as lower, inner, and upper canon is the same as in the original formation. Regarding the rule, the upper and the lower canon must be exchanged, but the lower canon with its sustained notes is a much better bass than the upper canon.

135

Seven-part triple canon in the major sixth or minor lower third.

The inner canon has six bars; the outer canons four bars.
The two upper canons ascend, the lower canon descends.

8
8
8
8

Canons in the major third and minor sixth

If the whole-tone scale in groups of two notes is uniformly harmonized, and if the progression of parts in these groups remains the same, then, in four-part setting, three-part canons in the minor third or minor sixth are the result, because the groups and their harmonzation are a major third apart. (Occasionally diminished fourths and augmented fifths will be seen instead of major thirds and minor sixths.)

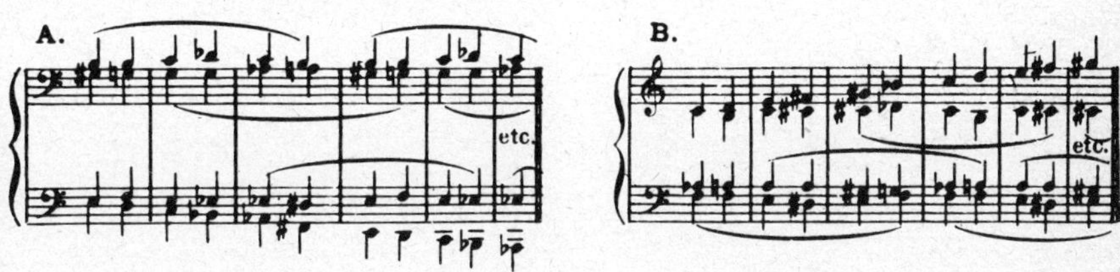

As a rule, sketches should be carried out in double-counterpoint as is shown in the following examples. If the scale remains fixed to a certain part, the other three parts can be exchanged in six different ways.

Elaboration of a sketch.

The chords here chosen are a diminished seventh-chord with a minor resolution, in symmetrical inversion with a major resolution.

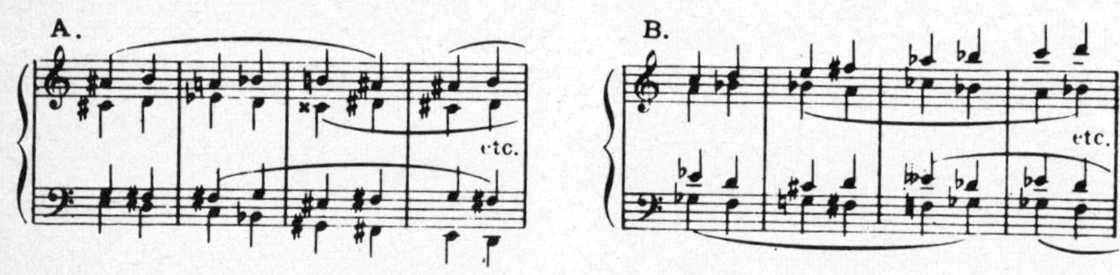

No doubt, as tedious as possible; but nevertheless a three-part canon. It becomes more agreeable through accidental dissonances, which are to be added in each group likewise.

Examples

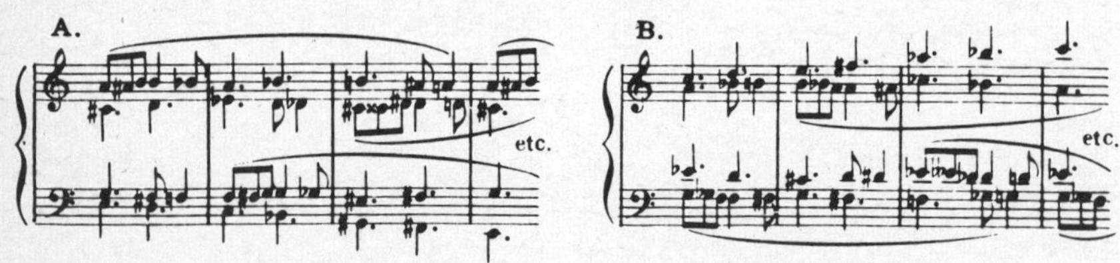

To make the theme melodiously more intersting another bar is required, containing a few leaps. The material is taken from the respective chords. This new bar is to be interpolated where it seems most appopriate; by this process the canon also receives one more part.

Examples

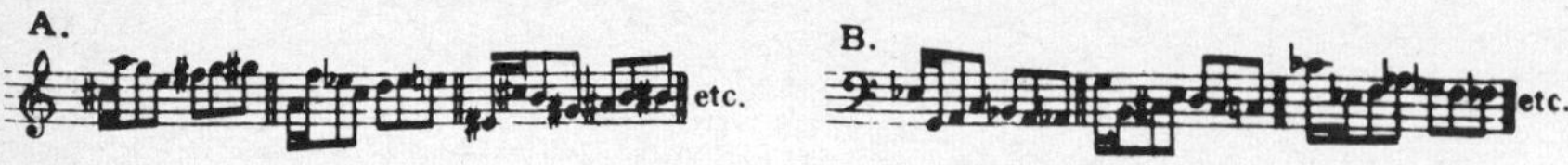

Every bar added lengthens the theme, and increases the number of parts. The figuration could be made richer, and an exchange of parts could take place at the beginning.

Example

Furthermore, if the scale is mingled with chordic tones it may be considered a new theme and elaborated canonically. A double-canon is the result. See the eight-part canon in this chapter.

A few more 2, 3, 4, and 5-part canons developed from the same sketch.

The part-progression more vivid from beginning.

Two-part canons.

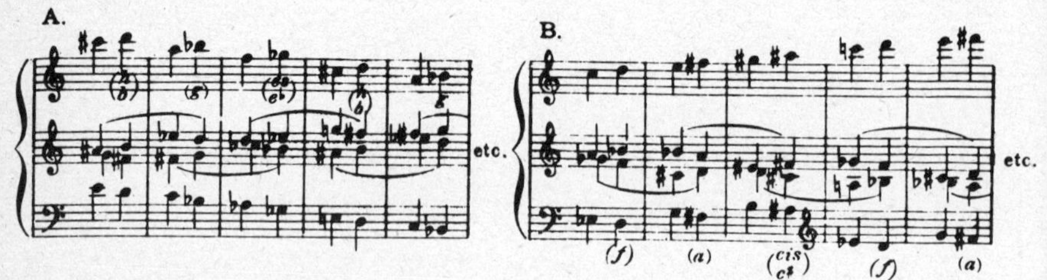

The upper part ornamented.

The theme still more vivid.

Three-part canons

The scale is ornamented

Four-part canons

The scale becomes part of the theme.

The parts enter after each other.

B.

etc.

The scale remains intact, and the theme is enlarged by one new bar.

(Free: the last eighth in the outer parts)

Five-part canons

Scale and theme united, and another bar added.

From the same ground three five-part double-canons evolved, given later on.

Two-part canons in the major third

Whole-tone scale and broken augmented triad accompanying.

A four-part canon in the major third with the whole-tone scale as accompaniment.

B

Two three-part canons in the major third

Theme of 6 bars

1.

The whole-tone scale with passing semitones accompanying.

2.

Double-canons in the major third

Chromatic double-canon in the major third.

Two five-part double-canons

B.

Two six-part double-canons in the major third

The four- and the two-part canons have four bars and descend; inverted they ascend.

8
8
B
8
8
8

8
8
8
8
8

Two six-part double canons in the major third

Both canons have four bars. The one of four parts ascends; the one of two parts descends; symmetrically vice versa.

B

Two seven-part double-canons in the major third.

The four-part canon has four bars and ascends; symmetrically it descends. The three-part canon has three bars and remains constant in pitch.

A.

B
8

Two eight-part double-canons in the major third or minor sixth.

(Compare p. 205 "Elaboration of a sketch") Both canons have four bars and ascend; symmetrically they descend. Free cadence: the last three chords.

B.
8

Two six-part double-canons of which the second half is the retrograde inversion of the first half.

The four-part canon• has four bars; the two-part canon two bars.

Omitting the two-part canon, the additional four-bar variation of the whole-tone scale can be taken as supplement to the four-part canon.

Retrograde inversion

free

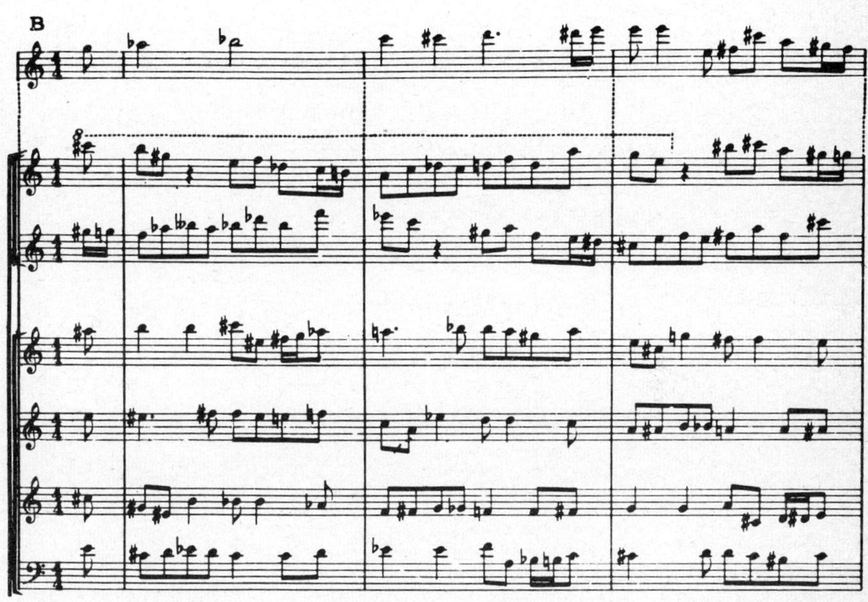
B
8

8

8
8

8
8
8
8

Canons in the tritone

If in a four-part setting the chromatic scale in groups of six, or the whole-tone scale in groups of three notes, is harmonized uniformly, and the part-progression in the different groups is not altered, three-part canons in the tritone, or its inversion, the diminished fifth, result.

(The half-tone scale may be interrupted by whole-tones, and the whole-tone scale by half-tones.)

A variation of the last two examples

A

B

A

B

The parts enter in succession

Two three-part canons in the tritone

The accompanying scale in canon A may be considered as E♭ major or A major. In both instances the scale is composed in the same manner: major with augmented fourth, minor sixth and seventh, and an additional minor second:

Consequently, in the symmetrical inversion, canon B, the scale is F# minor or C minor with minor second and major sixth, and an augmented fourth:

Two-part canons in the tritone are easily composed by harmonizing the whole- or half-tone scale in contrary motion. What is said above and in previous chapters about division in groups and alteration of the scale holds good here too.

A variation of these settings

Two accomplished examples

Two four-part canons in the tritone
Theme of 8 bars

A

free cadence

Rudimentary sketch

Chord progressions repeated in the tritone.

B

Two four-part canons in the tritone
Theme of 4 bars.

B

Two five-part canons in the tritone, with the chromatic scale as supplementary part.

Theme of unequal sections: ten bars divided seven and three. Two parts begin with the larger section, and three parts with the smaller one.

B

Six-part canon in the minor lower second or major seventh

Theme of 12 bars, of which the first two are taken from Mozart's 2nd C minor Fantasia.

(Minor second and major seventh are sometimes enharmonically disguised.)

8

adagissimo
rit.
(free cadence)
rit.
marcato
rit.
rit.
marcato
rit.

Six-part canon in the minor second or major lower seventh.

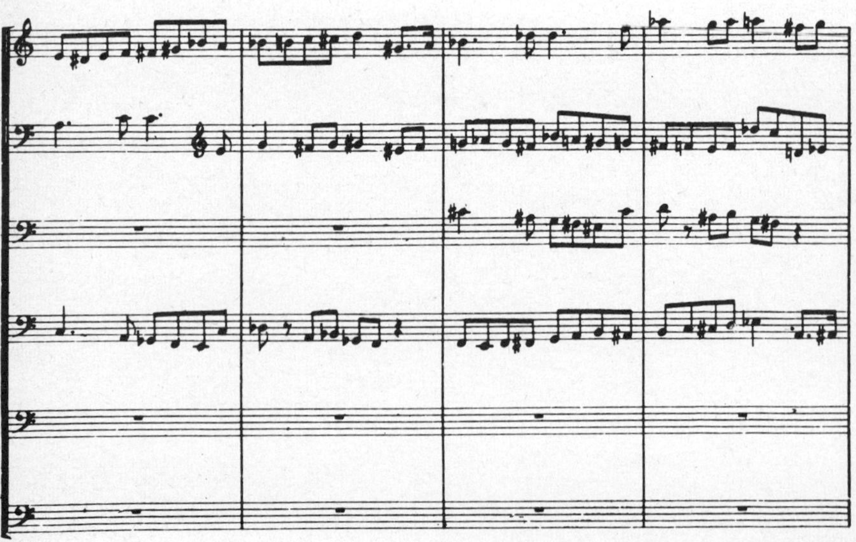

8

8

adagissimo
rit.
marcato
rit.
rit.
marcato
rit.
rit.

15 Canons on the Basso ostinato of the Crucifixus in Bach's B Minor Mass

1. A. 4 parts. In the "fifth and octave". Free cadence.
2. A. 4 parts. Tenor and soprano in contrary motion to bass and alto. Free cadence.
3. A. The same, but the theme but once in each part, and then free progression.
4. A. 4 parts. Alto and soprano in contrary motion to bass and tenor. Free cadence.
5. A. The same, but in other intervals.
6. A. 3 parts and a free one. Soprano in contrary motion to bass and tenor. Free cadence. The repetition may be ended where the hold is given, which serves as sign of closing only.
7. A. Two-part canon in the minor second with two free parts. In every part the second half is the symmetrical inversion of the first half. Free: the last note in the bass.

2. A.
2. B.
3. A.
3. B.
4. A.
4. B.

5. A.
5. B.
6. A.
1
2
6. B.
1
2

8. Four-part canon with two supplementary parts

The two upper parts are the sym. inv. of the two lower parts. The free inner parts are also symmetrically arranged. Consequently, the whole setting is its own symmetrical inversion.

Canonic elaboration of a short motive

Since hundreds of years, the motive here chosen is used frequently, but, to my knowledge, never canonically.

(*Heinrich Schütz*, Historie des Leidens und Sterbens, Nr. 21; *Georg Muffat*, 6., 7 and 11. Toccata; *Pergolesi*, Stabat Mater, Nr. 12; *Johann Sebastian Bach*, Fugue über "Jesus Christus, unser Heiland der von" — Musikalisches Opfer, Fugue 1, bar 133; *Wilhelm Friedemann Bach*, F minor Fugue in 3 voices; *Gluck*, Orpheus, Aria: Che farò senza Euridice: *Wagner*, Tristan, Sterbelied; *Robert Franz*, Op. 16, Nr 1-Op.51, Nr. 10; *Bruckner*, D minor Mass, Et incarnatus — 6th Symphony, 4th movement.)

I. a) in the lower part, b) in the upper part the theme twice in diminution.

II. Canon in the fourth, per thesin et arsin, meaning the parts enter on accented and unaccented beats. The upper parts in diminution.

No II as enigmatic canon

III. Canon in the major second, soprano and tenor in diminution, whereby in every second measure the theme appears in contrary motion.

IV. Canon in the minor third. Bass and alto in contrary motion. Soprano and tenor in diminution.
Soprano, 1st and 3rd bars: theme in contrary motion: 2nd and 4th bars: theme in original form. Tenor 1st and 3rd bars: theme retrograde; 2nd and 4th bars: theme retrograde in contrary motion.

V. The same construction as in no. IV, but the canon is in the fourth, and soprano and tenor are interchanged.

VI. The following six examples are canons in the minor second. The theme doubled by thirds or sixths, and a free part added. The last example with two free parts.

Symmetrical Canons

In canons of this kind the parts correspond symmetrically.

A sketch where alto and bass are the sym. inv. of the soprano and tenor.

In the following four elaborations of this sketch every repetition of the themes is altered, to show variety.

The upper parts exchanged, also the lower parts.

The next canon starts like the sketch given above, but soon the theme changes and becomes continuous.

Freely invented canon. Theme of 8 bars.

A variation of Carpenter's canon

B. Z.

A.

B.

Of the following symmetrical canon the second half is the retrograde inversion of the first half.

Symmetrical inversion

A six-part symmetrical canon

When all parts are in consent (sounding together) the sym. inv. does not bring forth anything that is not given in the original setting, because the parts having the same theme repeat it on the same degree. Therefore, the arrangement of parts may remain the same.

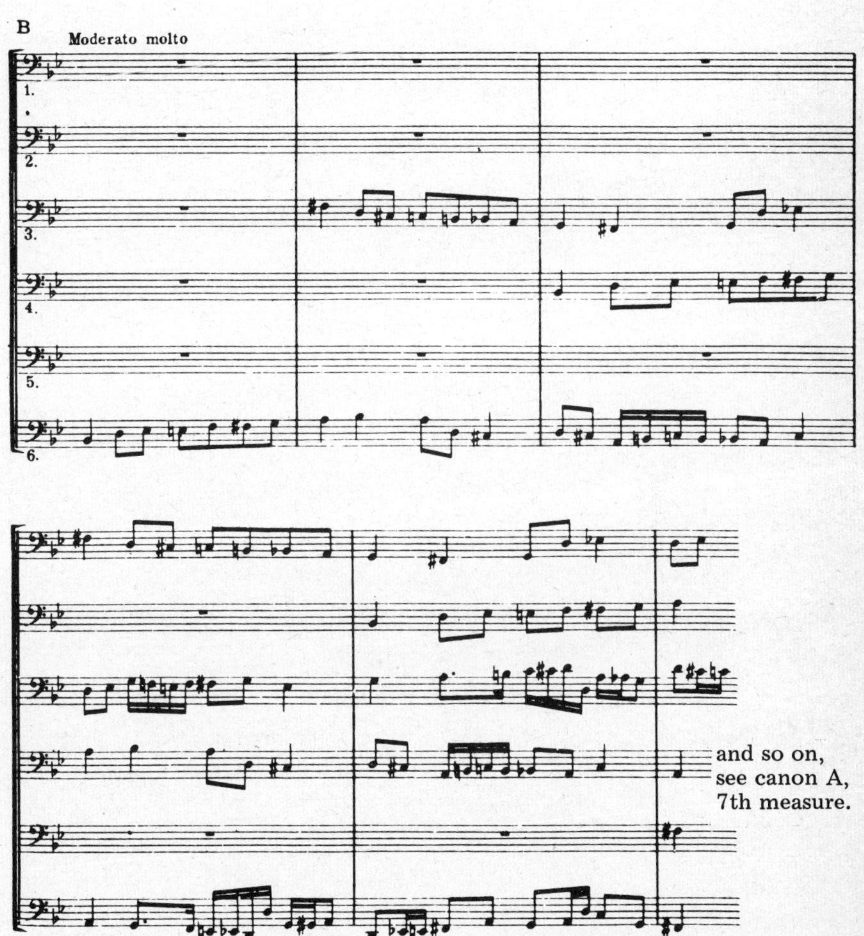

Symmetrical double-canons

Canons of this kind contain two different themes, both in original and in symmetrically inverted form. In the following four examples the inner parts correspond, and the outer parts likewise. Each theme is 6 bars long.

The 2nd theme begins

Symmetrical double-canons with continuous themes.

Symmetrical double-canon

In the Missa canonica by *J.J. Fux* the Agnus Dei begins with a two-part canon in the contrarium reversum for bass and soprano. (The two inner parts are supplements without the slightest imitation.)

With this canon another two-part canon can be combined, e.g.:

Album-Leaf

A symmetrical double-canon of which the symmetrical inversion is at the same time the retrograde inversion.

The tenor is the symmetrical inv. of the bass, and the soprano of the alto.

The alto is the retrograde inv. of the bass, and the soprano of the tenor.